CW00751382

BEAUTIFUL BLOOMS

A COLOURING BOOK
OF FLOWERS

chartwell
books

BEAUTIFUL BLOOMS

Brilliant flowers, vines of every stripe, glorious gardens galore, and more— *Beautiful Blooms* just begs for you to dive in and add your own spin on this bounty of blooms. Offering a wide range of gorgeous designs and scenes for you to personalize, these 100-plus stunning templates are perfect for relaxing after a serious session of weeding—or let them inspire you during the coldest months of the year.

Whether you have a green thumb—or you just wish you did—you can get your garden on and find your inner peace as you bring to life lush summer gardens and birds spreading their wings. Engage your mind and imagine a light spring breeze as you focus on the task at hand and colour the intricate patterns, flowers and foliage, stamens and pistils, and all manner of garden visitors, from butterflies to bumblebees.

Each piece of art is line drawn and ideal for coloured pencil, marker, or gel pen. On the back of each page are also intricate meditative patterns for you to colour and enjoy. By the end, you'll have gained beautiful, frameable works of art. And who knows? Maybe you'll end up following those creative instincts and taking them out into the garden.

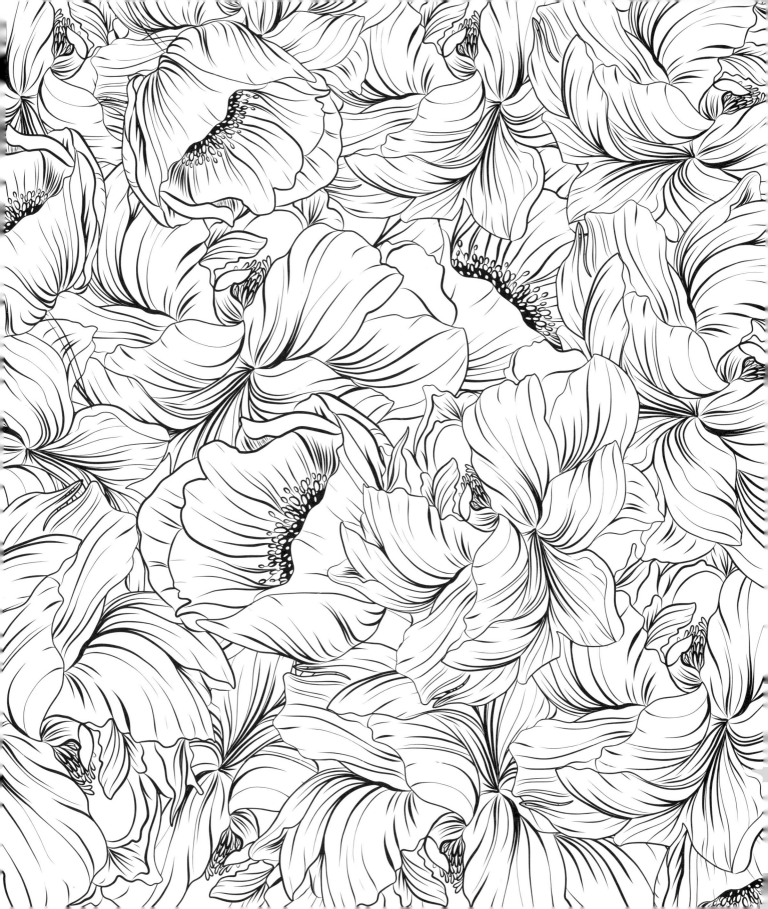

Brimming with creative inspiration, how-to projects, and useful information to enrich your everyday life, quarto.com is a favorite destination for those pursuing their interests and passions.

© 2022 Quarto Publishing Group USA Inc.

This edition published in 2022 by Chartwell Books, an imprint of The Quarto Group 142 West 36th Street, 4th Floor New York, NY 10018 USA T (212) 779-4972 F (212) 779-6058 www.Quarto.com

All rights reserved. No part of this book may be reproduced in any form without written permission of the copyright owners. All images in this book have been reproduced with the knowledge and prior consent of the artists concerned, and no responsibility is accepted by producer, publisher, or printer for any infringement of copyright or otherwise, arising from the contents of this publication. Every effort has been made to ensure that credits accurately comply with information supplied. We apologize for any inaccuracies that may have occurred and will resolve inaccurate or missing information in a subsequent reprinting of the book.

10 9 8 7 6 5 4 3 2 1

Chartwell titles are also available at discount for retail, wholesale, promotional, and bulk purchase. For details, contact the Special Sales Manager by email at specialsales@quarto.com or by mail at The Quarto Group, Attn: Special Sales Manager, 100 Cummings Center Suite 265D, Beverly, MA 01915, USA.

ISBN: 978-0-7858-4153-1

Publisher: Wendy Friedman
Editorial Director: Betina Cochran
Senior Design Manager: Michael Caputo
Editor: Jennifer Kushnier
Designer: Kate Sinclair

All stock design elements ©Shutterstock

Printed in China